Lydia Towsey is a poet expl⟨ heritage and her experience city of Leicester. She draws model to challenge the idea the way we look at ourselve⟨ ... other. Lydia has won a Decibel commission and been shortlisted for the Bridport Poetry Prize. She has spoken at the House of Lords and presented at Plymouth University's Zombie Symposium.

The Venus Papers

Lydia Towsey

Burning Eye

.

This edition published by Burning Eye Books 2015

www.burningeye.co.uk
@burningeyebooks

Burning Eye Books
15 West Hill, Portishead, BS20 6LG

ISBN 978 1 90913 658 8

Cover image by Scott Bridgwood
www.scottbridgwood.daportfolio.com

Dear Dr Sethi,
Thanks for your wonderful dentistry!

The Venus Papers

No poems about teeth
but one about a polar bear
and one about a shark...
both of which
have very good ones!

Thanks so much again —
you've made my smile, Lydia X

Contents

Not One of Those People

I'm not one of those English people pretending to be Welsh.
I do not speak the language. I do not understand
the landscape. Their weather systems – tearing through their
valleys, blasting their cliffs, bringing down their trees –
stagger me with their violence. My mother is Welsh;
she speaks yr Cymraeg – slips into it as easy
as umbrellas turned over in winter. When she finds a
Welsh bus driver, a new Welsh person working in her
local English corner shop, her English vowels are scrambled,
tongue clicks into new shapes and the Welsh she has no use for
is shaken out like a rolled-up bedspread – or a map – dust
rising up in cast-off clouds and settling silent as soft shoes.

Once, when I was six or eight, my mother was hoovering.
I was making a nuisance of myself;
wailing and crashing like a small ocean,
treading on the wires of my mother's tail, deliberately
getting in the way. My mother – turned the hoover off and
grabbed me by the waist, pulled me up, legs akimbo,
forced my arms around her damp-from-working vest and
sang to me. Words I didn't understand. Words that sounded
made-up. Words she had no use for. Words that slid like iron
from her lips and slapped against my skin like a cold and sunny day.
I couldn't sleep without them for months – not until I had them
hard-wired amongst my TV jingles and night-time prayers.

Sometimes – I would take this small fragment
of my mother's tongue to school
and recite it – over and over:

> *Gee ceffyl bach yn cario ni'n dau*
> *Dros y mynydd i hela cnau*
> *Dwr yn yr afon a cherrig yn slic*
> *Cwypo ni'n dau, wel dyna'i chi dric.*

The story of a horse
that fell into a river
and then
got up again.

I asked my mother to teach me Welsh,
to help me move my mouth in different ways,
to click and snap my lips, to talk about her
lost hills and valleys and weather systems,
to roll my words in earth – and salt – and rain.
We never got round to it.

The Don't Look Dance

On Sunday nights we would sit
in a paisley lounge with Coke and Lilt;
my mother would have a barley wine,
my father a beer or tomato juice

and we would watch
Hercule Poirot,
Miss Marple, Morse,
Inspector Wexford

and the light would bathe us
like a family of moles,
our coffee table like a tiny throne;
the frames on the walls would softly glow,
my brother and I in uniforms.

But my mother would sit on the edge of her seat
and as the music flickered to the murder scene
she would be up and on her feet,
closing the distance from sofa to screen,
holding her skirt like a crinoline shield,
        doing – the don't look dance.

My mother would do the don't look dance
in front of our analogue telly;
she'd hold up her skirt like a sunray,
her floral print for Marilyn's pleats.

And behind her skirt
was Captain Hastings,
a body in a stairwell,
blood on a carpet.

Behind her skirt
were the Brixton riots
and the miners' strike
and Chernobyl exploding.

My mother would do the don't look dance,
she would dance – the honolulu –

and anything with
shards or knives
or anything with blood
would be flowers or stripes
or polka dots –

something comfortable,
something good –

like the fish we'd had for lunch
with parsley sauce and mash

or the visit to Clarks
to measure our feet,
the coats she bought
to keep us clean

and in the evenings
the way she'd stand
in front of the screen

like a lunar eclipse,
        a disturbing dream.

        And behind her skirt
was Michael Buerk
in 1984 in Ethiopia.

        Behind her skirt
was the boy next door,
my grandma's dementia,
my brother's leukaemia.

My mother would dance
a Torvill and Dean
for famine and suffering
and war-torn fields.
My mother would do
        a   jazz   hands   shimmy
for malaria, typhoid
and malnutrition.

My mother would do
the don't look dance
in front of our bubble TV;
        she'd hold out her skirt

        like a fire curtain,

        her floral prints

        for Monroe's pleats.

She'd hide us from all of the hurting.
She'd cover the wounds of the world.
She'd fill that small room with her caring
but I never understood.

My mother would do   the don't look dance
the don't look dance   the don't look dance
My mother would do   the don't look dance
the don't look dance   the don't look dance
My mother would do   the don't look dance
but now   I can't look away.

The Visit

When my mother comes to visit she brings my dad
and a pack of twelve quilted Andrex toilet tissues,
half a pack of Weetabix and, since she has
started cutting down on dairy products,
a carton of rice milk. My mother brings
Lancôme samples she got from Boots –
white tubes inside of miniature packages
smaller than match boxes,
a tote bag she got as a free gift –
two purchases or more
from Christian Dior;
she saved for the foundation
with her pension
and housekeeping.
When I move into my flat
my mother brings me a plant,
she brings me a card –
two mice in tiny clothes,
'Good Luck in Your Home';
when I get my degree
a card from them both;
when he leaves the room
a twenty-pound note.
'Don't tell your dad.'
She brings me a scarf made of lace,
cystitis powders – just in case.
She brings me a jar of
thick-cut orange marmalade
bought from the woman
who lives round the corner,
a top from Marks she had on order
and a cut-out coupon
from Woman's Weekly.

I bring my mum
a cup of tea.
No sugar.
Milk.

Cheese on Toast at 2am

Sweep of the salt, the sauce, the grill,
toasting – the rarebit
of the evening one recalls:

Cariad – Arian – Ach-y-fi –

three crows
black against the grit
of the night-time;

Darling – the money –
my mother curses at the sink.

The Hungarians on the other side
throw their luggage over starboard
and climb the ladder to the sea.

Alice

When I first met Alice

I asked her where she'd come from –
she told me Butare

in Rwanda,

'Rwanda,'

she said.

'Genocide?'

Alice   plays the drums in Rwanda
        which is taboo if you're a girl –
                she can tap out a beat
        with the soles of her feet
                or hammer it into the face of a pail.

Alice   teaches me

        the Dance of Seduction –

teaches me Rwandan
for saying   I love you,

'Nda

gukunda,'

then   the significance   of the cow.

'When you dance
                the Dance
of Seduction
                you must make your arms
like the horns   of a cow.
                Your eyes   should be wide
like a cow's.
                You must move
and turn   and roll your chest   like a cow.'

In Rwanda
dowries are paid

and families are fed
on cows.
                I must not worry, she says:

I   –   have the voice   –   of a cow

                      and this is a start.
We do not talk
              about Rwanda's genocide.
We do not talk
              about Butare
where Alice lived.
            Where no one came.
                  Where genocide
did not   exist.
            We drink   tea.
We just sit here
           drinking tea.

Hospital

In this place
there is more tea
than there is water
in the sea.

Miss Havisham's House

She sleeps in a cupboard
upright and awkward,
talks to the planter
the elephant says,

drinks tea
from a see-through saucer;
shoebox of sparrows,
pillar-box fez.

Ms Rochester visits
on Tuesdays and Thursdays
to play all the records
and lie on the bed.

Come evening she marks
the passage of hours
by counting the bones
in a crocodile's head.

She writes long letters
on Victorian ledgers
to the great white bear
and the purple grouse.

A rail of veils
brilliant as washing
pushes off
like a first dance.

Once, she spots him
moving by the boxes,
radios up
to the moon in the loft.

She gazes – then squints
through a horn-rimmed
magnifier.

By the time they arrive
      he's always gone.

Little Song

Snails were eaten by the Romans and they introduced many varieties into Britain, which eventually spread.[1]

And when they came they came with Romans
in boats and crates like papers curled
but their shells were heavier than omens
and their ships set down like sighs unfurled.

And when they came they wanted to like it
but they didn't like the weather or the food
and they couldn't speak the language or make fit
what they had needed with the hostile mood.

Now each snail is a shell full of longing,
each garden a clearing of betrayal,
each ocean is a chasm of aching
for a snail that would drown if it tried to sail.

And this is their sadness, what all snails learn;
their home's on their back – but they can't return.

[1] Snail City: http://www.zephyrus.co.uk/ediblesnails.html

Long Black Coat

The time I took a taxi back from Nottingham,
night flying by in dizzying squares of blackness,
foreign landscape usually only glimpsed from trains,
I rang you on my mobile – drunk, voice slurring consonants.
You were pissed off but needn't have done a thing.
Except – when the car slid into Leicester station
you were there, striding with a purpose towards us –
your long black coat, looking like a boxer or a bear,
hair wild from sleep, face pale as moonlit water. You
paid the man and caught me, falling through the door, to
half-carry me through the early hours of morning
back to yours and there – you laid me down on fabric,
your soft brown curls, pale face, cold hands – all mixed up and
saying nothing. Your long black coat   inside my head.

Sunday Afternoons

My mother used to fall asleep on Sunday afternoons.
I only remember now I've done the same.
She used to lie down on the sofa –

fully clothed and hands like roots around her face,
fingers pink from doing dishes, washing windows,
lifting bags without her gloves.

On arriving home from church
my mother would remove elasticated waists,
carefully fold her floral tops, swap for T-shirts
threaded bare about the breast.

My mother used to fall asleep on Sunday afternoons
but she would leave her stockings on,
thick black nylon cloaking legs.

I think my mother sometimes dreamt.
We'd sometimes hear her
murmur through her teeth.

Once I drew her – art coursework, Foundation Degree:

      coal feet,
      clubbed and crushed from Sunday heels.

Now
I fall asleep on Sunday sofas –

wake to mumble, what time is it?
Light dimmed, limbs stiff.

I wake remembering I've dreamt of sex;
my body that was born from hers.

I wonder if she ever did the same.

Tawanda

Tell me about South Africa.
    What do you want to know?
Anything, I tell him.
Whatever I should know.

He's the friend of a friend,
we've not met before,
we've driven to this pub,
he's meeting as a favour

and we've sat down
like we're on a date,
him in his work clothes,
me in my lipstick.

I've bought him a drink
and thanked for his time,
he's told me 'no problem',
we've sketched out our lives.

I've poured in my tonic,
he's sipped at his tea,
I've unpacked my notebook –
he's looking at me.

And his hair is a mountain,
a black woollen ridge,
his shirt's made from cotton
against his dark skin.

Tell me about South Africa.
    What do you want to know?
Whatever you can tell me.
Whatever I should know.

He comes from Zimbabwe
but he's lived in Jo'burg,
he's got family in Cape Town,
friends in Soweto.

South Africa is a massive subject,
to say it all
we'd be here all night
but he can tell me,
he says
as he watches me nod,
something, he says
as he watches me write.

You can't talk about all this
without talking apartheid;
separate toilets for blacks,
restaurants, street signs.

You couldn't live in Jo'burg,
your place was in the townships.
You couldn't learn your language –
Xhosa, Sotho, Tsonga...

and you couldn't drink their beer
and he gestures to the bar,
you couldn't do their jobs,
as the jukebox plays guitar,

and all this was maintained
by dividing up to conquer;
different rights for Asians,
different rights for coloureds.

A homeland was stolen
while nobody was looking.
School children were murdered,
gunned down just for questioning.

Tell me about South Africa.
What do you want to know?
Whatever you can tell me.
Whatever I should know.

And the rain is on the window,
the night outside is drawing in,
he gets a pint of Stella,
I get another gin.

> I could tell you how it's hard
> now everything is better;
> I could talk about the crime,
> the lack of education,
>
> but South Africa is beautiful,
> the land goes on forever,
> it's hot and flat and dry
> but more than just the weather.
>
> Spend a night in Cape Town
> where the land is on the sea.
> Spend a night in Franschhoek
> with its cellars and its trees.
>
> Tell you about South Africa,
> I'll tell you what I know,
> I'll tell you of our mountains,
> I'll tell you of our malls.

And he talks about his uncle
who got rich with a truck,
who when apartheid ended
made money with some sand.

He talks about the barbecues
that happen in the townships,
how when the weekend comes
everyone goes back there.

> It doesn't matter what your car is;
> you'll go back to Mzoli,
> you'll sit out in the sun
> and drink and talk and party.

And as we're sitting in this pub,
he says he'll never get it,
how the English go to bars
and sit inside till closing.

      In South Africa it's different;
      you'll drive out to the store,
      you'll park up in the car park,
      you'll drink out on your car,

      you'll sit out on your bonnet,
      you'll hang out with your friends,
      you'll listen to your music,
      you'll watch the sun descend.

And as we're driving from the pub,
as he drives me to the station,
he asks me what I do
when I go out in Leicester.

As mbira fills the stereo
he describes its tiny keys.
As the rain falls on the windshield
the music slips beneath our feet.

      Talk about South Africa,
      I'll talk about the jazz
      that fills the night like hope,
      that makes you understand.

He asks me when I'm reading
this poem that I'm writing;
as I'm walking to the trains
he calls to me – I'll come there.

Tell me about South Africa.
      What do you want to know?
Whatever you can tell me.
Whatever I should know.

Jamaican Love Song

After T.S. Eliot, 'The Love Song of J. Alfred Prufrock'.

Let us go and sit outside
upon this wide veranda,
where mangoes grow
and palm trees sway
and orange flowers
bloom like flames.
Let's draw some coffee
from this pot
and sip it gently
while we watch
the cars slip by
like ballerinas,
wires stretch
like metal creepers.
Across the road
let's see the sea
that softly glows
like someone's dream.
Let's see the sea
behind the bar
already open
like a barn
built like a box
from paper wood,
its sign hung up,
its cotton hood.
Let us sit here in the shade,
watch the children run and play –
the woman in her godly hat,
her shining arms behind her back.
Let us go down roads that burn,
down sunlit streets and sit in bars
where people meet
and drink away the afternoon
and talk to people, buy a cue

of vodka, rum or Malibu.
Let us drive down narrow lanes,
watch the children run and play,
the children with their bellies heavy,
children waiting, children ready.
Let us go, let us see
the man with dust upon his feet,
the woman with the cataracts,
the farmer walking with his axe.
Let us go, let us see
the factory that went to sleep,
the company that didn't stay
when tax incentives went away.
The smell of rain,
the smell of meat –
I think I'll run along the beach,
I think I'll sit,
I think I'll sleep,
I think I'll walk,
I think I'll creep.
It doesn't matter what you do;
the sky gets dark
and then the moon.
Let us go now,
let us go
where mangoes grow
and palm trees sway.
Let us go
where flowers flame.
Let us go,
let us go
and in the ocean
write our name.

Eton Boys

Now this is the winter of our discontent
we shall wait with weight upon our heads –
We've made a list of calculations,
say Eton-educated men.

The elderly must sell their houses,
women learn to stay at home –
the public sector doesn't need you,
we only had it on a loan.

Disabled children lose their bedrooms,
immigrants are left to bleed
as nurses learn they've no compassion
and teachers' hands are tied to teach.

Now this is the winter of our discontent
we shall wait with weight upon our heads –
Hurts us just as much as you,
say Eton-educated men.

Hospitals are shaved with scapulas,
students work from age sixteen,
abandon all ye education,
learn to parrot dates and scenes.

Abandon college for a factory,
learn to work and feed machines;
the system has a need of people
to push the train that oils the wheels.

Now this is the winter of our discontent
we shall wait with weight upon our heads –
Yours is not to question why,
say Eton-educated men.

The country has a brand new boys' club
made for banks and billionaires;
leave your bullion at the cloakroom
to be laundered, stoked and freshly aired.

The sick are signed up to the work force
as idleness should never pay.
If you are rich and very wealthy
we hope that you enjoy your stay.

Now this is the winter of our discontent
we shall wait with weight upon our heads –
The poor are often undeserving,
say Eton-educated men.

Night Train

And the night would creep like jasmine gently
and the light would fade like blackened ribs,
they'd lie on the bed like lovers carefully
and the moon would silver curled-up limbs.

And the leaves would press the dark glass lightly
and they'd look with palms like held-up eyes,
the cats outside would scrape past softly
and they'd hear their bells like hopeful cries.

These were the times they'd later think of
when all that they were had passed like snow;
that they'd shuffled songs and combed the hours,
how they'd loved each other but always known.

A saxophone had played like a night train
and the wind had murmured – leaves, sighs, dust, rain.

Yucca

My yucca plant is happy.
It has taken my central heating
for Central America.

It believes my lava lamp
to be a visitation
from a tropical sun god.

It grows confidently,
strong in the belief
that my erratic pattern of watering
is consistent with flash flooding.

My yucca plant is happy
high above its carpet plain,
with the TV setting in the evening
and the car birds calling
far off beyond its canopy.

My ivy plant
hangs its leaves
along the bookcase.

It tells my yucca
it is just a yucca.

But my yucca does not listen.
It knows that the ivy is mad.

Love Poem to a Polar Bear

After 'The Passionate Shepherd to His Love' by Christopher Marlowe.
For Peppy, the taxidermied Fox's Glacier Mints polar bear.

Come live with me and be my love,
Dear Polar Bear like snow-white glove,
And if you need a place to sleep
I'll build for you an icy keep.

I'll sneak you past the concierge
Who sleeps and dreams of polar bears
And we can take the stairs or lift
Just like we're climbing up a drift.

And on my floor that's number two
We'll swim like divers to my rooms:
The lounge that's painted like a cave,
The arctic bathroom that I've made.

And when it's cold you'll think it's nice
And when it thaws I'll buy you ice
And you can have your own soft seat
And a stool to rest your feet.

There in my flat I'll feed you cake,
Silver squares of frosted Flake,
And in my freezer I'll keep cod;
Come live with me and be my love.

Dear Polar Bear, I'll leave those men
Who call at eight and nine and ten;
I'll be with you, my number one.
Come live with me, my Polar Love.

From Italy with Love

I love to come home in the summer
and find in the bright case of the cold fridge
the cool, white, dense ball of the buffalo mozzarella –
the bomb of it – closed in its bag on the shelf in the door
or in the salad compartment – as calm and perfect as a
hard-boiled egg – a message from your ex – sent via the
supermarket from Italy. I love its planetary mass – blank face,
murmuring milk, the ivory slash of its veiled dress as I scissor
the seam of its printed plastic, pour the suspense of its water into
the sink. I love its cold dish. There is nothing better than to take
a knife to it. To cut clean – pare into moist, firm, impenetrably
celled opaque slices – to salt it, vinegar it, take by the horns
of its soft bulk – drizzle with the thickest syrup of olive green,
drown out and pacify its fist, nothing more than between me
and it. Nothing better than to peel off its skin, lift up each
forkful – glinting in the quiet light of the summer kitchen –
bird song streaming through the window. Nothing better
than to gaze, undo, defuse – neutralise, forget –
make safe as an oyster, the silken sigh of its dissent;
amore, amore, e morte, then – guzzle, tear, lick,
slip down the gullet. Nothing better.
Devour. Finito. Ex.

Let's Not Say Love

like love's a frog,
a silver slipper.
Let's not say love
like love's a lane.
Let's not say love
like love's confetti,
like every paper heart
will magic up a wedding,
my mother in a hat,
your auntie with a handkerchief.
Let's not say love
like – every – single – minute,
like love is all we think of
till love is just a piece
of worn-out carpet on a stair.
Let's not say love
like love will cancel single,
like love is just a jingle,
like saying love
is all we need to do.
Let's not say love
because we said
that time before
after wine and maybe more
or late at night in bed,
'I love you,'
and now we think we can't go back
and every time you make me tea
I can't even count to three:
I love, I love, I love –
let's not say love
because we think it's nice,
because we think we might
unite –
before we're really sure?
Let's not say love
before I've let you in the door

to places I don't show,
the way I act when I'm alone.
Let's not say love
until we've seen each other cry,
until we've seen each other find
a way to show we really love,
until the love has set up home
and painted all our ceilings gold.
Let's not say love
in case it hears
and goes.

A Shark Called Lydia

Lydia the shark was tagged by OCEARCH in Jacksonville, Florida, on 2 March, 2013. She is the first great white to be seen crossing from one side of the Atlantic to the other, swimming just 700 miles off the coast of Devon. Those tracking her believe her to be either pregnant or looking to breed.

The other night I dreamt I was a shark.
As I lay in bed dead to the dark,
spread between sheets
like a crime scene
painted at the bottom of the sea,
my head filled with water.

I have never liked the water,
always had a terror of sharks,
a particular horror so that every sea
is a bath full of fins filling the dark,
every swimming pool a scene
from *Jaws*. The rain screams sheets,

hammerhead lashes and soaks the sheets,
behind my eyes a forest of kelp thickens the water.
In a morbid mirror I'm grey and white; picture the scene:
a pearly ridge protrudes from my back; I am a shark
clear as my nose that has grown enormous in the dark,
and round; pregnant as a pregnant – sea.

A newborn pup flees from its mother into the sea
to escape being eaten immediately, no wrapped in sheets
and presented black eyes blinking against the dark
Get out of the water!
It's a shark!
Here is the scene

with the murderous shark, the scene
with Medea drowning her children, smash of the sea.
Everyone always blames the mother.
But here in the night, a child is hanging from a twisted sheet.

A boy is still and staring from beneath the water.
A girl is pointing accusingly from the dark.

I have never liked the dark,
always feared the scene
with the basket on the sea,
the cries from the wicker carried on the water.
Nobody knows the heart of a shark;
its impossible numbers, pages, sheets.

In the silent dark of the bright night a silver scene opens on a sea;
a white shark walks upon the water waving a flag blank as a sheet
at a child who stands waiting, watching from a moonwashed beach.

Hungary

I saw a sign at the top of Rákóczi utca,

'Hungaroring – 2km';

                    this is a hungry body.

I devour the map of my grandmother's country,
utter its street names, recite its parks.

Said the Hungary ghost to the phantom famished,
'We walked all day with barely a sandwich.'

My grandma said nothing
and reclined in a room.

All of the road signs are written in algebra
or Latin and Ottoman shuffled cards.

Tables dance in alleys and avenues;
a little rain mists down.

There are no hippos in the River Danube
of either the plastic or the Hasbro variety.

There is no damage to Heroes' Plaza.
There are bullet holes on Lehel utca.

We took a metro to find the building,
szegény lélek – hungry ghost,

Erkel, Raday, Andrassy, Vaci –
                    roads switch names
when you move in close.

Great-grandmother crosses Rakosi's border
as he and her cousin were lovers in youth.

Great-grandma Rostos and the doctor
are turning the corner to Jozsef Korut.

We sat in the door of the church by Kapolna
as a bent-over women passed with a case.

We followed the water over to Castle
where Uncle Zoltán was fastened to Flóra
and pushed in the Danube shot in the head.

Kleptomania of architecture.
Quadrophenia of lights.
Obsessive-compulsive statue collector
dreaming roads once owned by empire.

Dracula paces in the Labyrinth of Buda,
Vlad the Impaler; sulphur-clouded, gothic-arched.

'Latvia, Austria, Slovakia, Bulgaria –
Old Hungary...'
         says the old woman
brushing her hair
in the antiques shop.

I map the devour of my grandmother's Hungary,
Bolivian bulimia of pathways and doors.
         I grandma devour the map of the hungry,
cavernous castles, amnesiac halls.

There are no hippos in the River Danube.
There are no homeless beneath the bridge.
There are no tin cans left to salvage.
There are no shelters left to sleep.

There are no rights for Romani people.
There is no place for same-sex love.
There is no freedom in the media;
publish and be damned, so hold your tongue.

I'm walking the streets
with the ghosts of relations,
         replaying histories
of rewound repeats.

There's no opposition in the National Assembly.
There's a man with a mandate playing king.

I'm walking the streets
through the warmth of the autumn,
holding the hem
of my grandmother's dress.

I'm walking the streets
with the heat on the pavement,
swastika sprayed
on the synagogue brick.

Hungary for Hungary.
No hungry in Hungary.

Hungary autocracy.
Forgetful democracy.

Hungry for Hungary,
my grandma is thirsty.

I'm crossing the reference,
bending the back,
turning the page,
reading the map,
tracing the script

of my grandmother's book.

October

Pizza, bruschetta, gold dress, Rioja;
autumn is here and winter forgotten,
walking through town arm in arm with a lover,
moon in the sky and leaves good as rotten.
The air is cool with the stench of roses;
I hold his hand – hosanna, incanto.
Autumn is here, drink coffee in cafés,
wine in bars, sashay in slips, tights and scarves.
Everything is fallen, there is rain on the street,
there is light on the path, the memory of heat.
Pizza, bruschetta, gold dress, Rioja;
summer is dead. Long live the autumn.

From Switzerland with Love

My Hungarian uncle
rings my cousin
from Switzerland.

> Sarah, it is me – Bandi.
> I have been talking to your father.
> I am worried about you.

Outside my uncle's living room
the slanting sides of snow-caked roofs
glitter fondant through the windows.

> Your father tells me
> you have broken up
> with your boyfriend.
> Ack! Sarah – I know
> a wonderful Cantor;
> yes, yes, here in Bern...

My cousin   blinks three times
                as though
            confetti flakes

        are tumbling

from out   the phone.

Bandi Bácsi,
what are
you talking about?

> A Cantor,   says my uncle,
> a Hazzan, a Chazzan –
> in our synagogue he leads the choir,
> he teaches the Mitzvah,
> he reads the Torah,
> he lights the candles,
> he chants the Kaddish, the Shema.

He is – a l i t t l e o l d e r – than you
but very handsome.

Bácsi, says my cousin –

> I have told him all about you.
> He will come and visit you in London.
> If you don't like him, no problem.

In Bern snow swirls.
A sugar-coated, trousered groom
pirouettes and croons a psalm.

My uncle Bandi
polishes his glasses,
pours water from the pot,
stirs sugar anti-clockwise,
removes the teaspoon from the cup.

My uncle
who breathes the minutes
of a second hand

taps the casing of a hunter's back,
listens for the skitter of the turning cogs,
the pulling of the movement,
the ratchet and the drum.

The hours in my uncle's house
are set by the meridian.
My uncle waits
for the rising of the sun,
the midnight barking of his dog,
the passing of the tram,
the knocking of his door
by his lover, Maryse.

My cousin –
      sends a stack
      of sequined seconds
      down the wire
      that turns like weather.
      Her eyes are dials.
      Her back is sprung.
      A key the colour of London rain
      fits between her shoulder blades,
to wind the wheels
inside the rings
inside the hoops
inside her head
that tick like hands
to twist the rest.

My cousin sighs
     for her body's tock,
            running with the
                   accuracy
                       of a Swiss
                           watch.

Bandi Bácsi, she says
and cracks a smile
from quarter past nine
to ten past ten.

Bandi Bácsi, she says...

As the snow pipes ice white.
As the moon-faced evening starts to chime.
As a klezmer band picks up a set
inside my uncle's kitchenette –

Bandi Bácsi, she says...
                  NO!
                       No!
                              no.

A Woman

After 'A Hand' by Jane Hirshfield.

A woman is not a monthly contract writ in blood.

Nor a motorway of arteries,
not the gardens of her lungs,
not the suitcase of her ribs,
not her boxing glove of heart,
not her marrow or her gut,
nor her stomach or her lips.

A woman is not a set of dots.

Nor the pixels on a page,
not the loaded butter knife of paint applied to canvas,
not the chilly marble of a chiselled statue.

A woman is not the ticking of a clock.

Not a pendulum or carriage,
not a red jewelled case,
nor an hourglass waiting out its sand.

She is not an advert for detergent,

nor a way for selling cars,
her breasts not metaphors for cans
nor melons.

Where is the woman?

On the board?
In the band? With the bank?
On the money?

Where is the woman?

In the school?

In the government?

Where is the woman?

Behind the lens?
Down the pub?
On the street?

Interview with a Barbie

Do you ever get tired of smiling?
In the street do passers-by say –
A: Frown!
B: But, Barbie – you're
anatomically incapable of walking.
Your torso's far too small to hold in all your organs.
You should be moving on fours, given your proportions.
Your waist's the same circumference as your head! Or –
C: Barbie, do you plan to kill again?

Did you ever wonder why you couldn't age?
Or why your heels were all so high?
Or why, though your favourite food is burgers
and you love to bake,
you never seem to eat
or put on any weight?
Barbie, is that murder in your eyes...

or are you just thinking about Ken?
And – how is the sex?
I wouldn't want to pry
but the lack of any bits
makes me think that you must
do it in some – special way?

Did you ever consider a
career in academia
but note the lack
of an accessorising attaché case?

And that there are few Football Barbies,
Army Barbies, Banker Barbies
or Barbies working on the stock exchange –
but you can be a (Class) President Barbie, or
Veterinary Surgeon Barbie –
as long as you keep it pink.
Or Mermaid Barbie. Or grow a pair
of wings...

Barbie, is that murder in your eyes
or are you checking in? Barbie –
have you ever considered

(more) plastic surgery
and wished (if only)
there was an online
child-friendly app to help?

Are you thinking about Ken?
Are you thinking about hairstyles?

Barbie... is that *a head* in your handbag?
A leg – jutting out the fridge?

Are you thinking about pets?
Are you thinking about travel?

Is that *blood* on the curtain?
In the shower? In the Dreamhouse?
In the Barbie Mariposa Princess Fairy Castle
on the butterfly-accented bedstead
and balconette and chandelier,
sprayed on the canopy,
the dressing table,
mirror set,
the limited
edition wallpaper
and ball-gowns
and twinsets
and rollers
and lipstick
accessories...
Running.
Pooling.
Splattered.
Barbie? ...Barbie?

...Babs?

!

In Praise of My Legs

Pillars. Scissors. Solid to their middles,
sticks of rock, printed with my mother's
maiden name, Edwards – potatoes –
playground chant sung for
knobbly knees, skippety wickets,
rickety from rickets – *she was raised
in a sweet shop* – fed on jars of
liquorice allsorts and sherbet lemons.
I have my mother's laugh
and my mother's legs –
they have their flaws:
tiled, carpeted,
lino, paved.
Boughs, beams,
turned, shaped.
My legs run like ship-masts,
lift up the sails of my hips
to fall from the crest
of their iliac wave,
noble as whale bones,
sheer as cliffs,
walk me strident,
drumstick defiant
to the shops,
to the park,
to the pub
through the rain,
candy-striped
and white with sun
flashing   brilliant,
run, dance, bend
through the hours,
days, weeks,
years.
My mother.
My mother.
My legs.

Amen.

I Shall Say

because
my mother always said –
'Don't'

because of her mother
and her mother
and her mother.

Because
the tiny woman enveloped
behind my clavicle –

bespectacled and floral,
sipping tea, smelling of lavender,

keeping budgerigars
heavy as bowling balls

hidden in handbags,
pressing her knitting on my diagrams,

her shopper on my diaphragm –
backing away from my

foo-foo, ya-ya
hoo-ha, fancy fish,
Bermuda triangle –
quick as she
Could Cod!
can can
says –

'Don't.'

Because

in a life-drawing class
of fifteen women and one man
fifteen people left a gap...

a white expanse –
between the thighs
and beneath the navel,

a question mark
like a fig leaf on an angel,

a peninsula of blank paper
in a sea of shading,

a unanimous moment of
eyes failing –

anchored on the magnet
of the same point.

Because
they are in sore need of a PR agent.

Because
there is a disparity between

poems about them
and poems by them.

Because pornography
has the monopoly.

Because
they are better than that.

Because
upstanding members,

dramatic potential,
expletive essential.

Because
they are beautiful

and though they can be harmful
and violent and brutal

I choose to believe
they are designed for love.

Because I wish
to reclaim them.

Because you've got to know
how to handle them.

Because some things are hard
but not impossible to talk about:

Cockatoo, Cock-a-hoop, Cockatiel, Coq au vin,
Cocktail, Cockpit, Cock-a-leekie, Cockermouth,
Coxon, Cock and bull, Coccyx, Cockroach,
Cock robin, Cockney, Cocked up, Cockfight,
Cock-sparrow, Cook-a-doodle, Cocksfoot, Cock-stride,
Cockatrice, Cockermamie, Cockabully, Cocker spaniel,
Cocky, Cockle, Cock-crow, Cock-snapper,
shuttleCock, ballCock, bibCock, weatherCock,
moorCock, peaCock, petCock, poppyCock,
woodCock, seaCock, unCock, stopCock,
Cock, Cock, Cock, Cock, Cock, Cock, Cock, Cock,
Cock, Cock, Cock, Cock, Cock, Cock, Cock, Cock,
Cock,   Cock,   Cock,   Cock,   Cock,   Vagina.

Badlands

We were in a Badlands bar when we heard the news
that Valentino Rossi was dead. 2am
and the air was thick with heat and cicadas;
we were drinking – tinto de verano and
cerveza, chunks of chorizo topping bread and
left untouched, TV blaring from a bracket
beyond a ribboned doorway. The barman told us
mistaking us for Italian, crossing the plaza
to stand between tables – 'Esse morto.'
Then in Spanish – 'Está muerto.'
Then in English – 'Dead.'

Badlands –

breakneck country packed with gorges and canyons
Martian red and lunar grey. Earlier that day
we'd come down the mountain, tin black car reflecting rays
descending from Cazorla, carrying water
in bottles like icemen filled up from fountains
to plunge into lakes.

Badlands –

electricity dead – the place we were staying
miraculous, wonderful – strung with a sun-roof
but missing its lights – and a fridge.

Badlands –

perilous country – made of sierras and
butter-knifed hill tops sliced and smoothed like loaves of bread,
pock-marked and cratered with black lichen and carpeted
conifers ragged with rocks.

Follow the road – over yellow-brick gullies,
ravines, precipices, dotted lines of corn-plait
trees and burning bushes. Stray dogs – keep to the villages,
cling to the light of the bars, beg for
scraps – bark at the dark.

We were in a Badlands bar when we heard the news.

An English woman who knew nothing of Rossi,
drowning her dreams in a jug of Rioja,
sun-baked skin and disappointed gaze – her Spanish
child wheeling her bike and drinking orange – nothing to do
but admire the view and shuffle the money
saved for rain.

Badlands –

no country for young men,
land carved out by wind and weather shaped by the
elements over millennia of time, blown
in from other hemispheres – *prohibido*
el paso – nothing personal...

but this air has travelled   and it's come a long way,
blown in from Morocco, scirocco, Somalia,
the Ivory Coast – migrant labourers peddling
ripped CDs and cheap sunglasses, packets of tissues,
T-shirts and watches, traveling   from the sub-Saharan,

then from town to town, village to village,
35°C in the shade to be looked away from
and dismissed with a shrug?

In these Badlands, Madlands – made of midday sun that
sinks at night to wrap the heights in veils of shade,

this   land   owes   you   nothing

and the mountains spread like painted fans and sigh for
water that never comes, or when it does   can
only run down folded arms of lime and sand,
volcanic rock, rigid and lined, impervious
to touch.

High up in the altitude   tidelines run like stretch-marks
water-damaged in the flood – you can still see stars,
you can still see scars – you can still see shells
if you look hard enough

in these Badlands –

where rocks run on in coloured ridges that seem to
bleed – tinto de verano   through arid fingers

and land once made by gushing water is now as
dry as a reformed alcoholic, just the
occasional lapse   for a man-made lake   or a
Neolithic   aqueduct.

We were in a Badlands bar when we heard the news.

Forget about Rossi –

even here, remotest of villages – half of
the houses are bought up by tourists, to be
visited as rarely as an unpopular
relative.

Farmhouses stand like the last survivors
with whitewashed walls and blown-off rafters,

deserted machinery's left for the rushes,
combine harvesters turning the dust up

and the young people leave.

Badlands –

where the sun beats down like *Unforgiven* and
shimmers and sears and bends the road beneath the windshield.

Should you spit on the ground it will spit like an egg

and sizzle away before you've licked your lips
and without this car we'd die of exposure
and nobody would know or find the bodies,
leopard skin wrapped with yellow sand and dotted shrubs
cannot change its spots   while the road runs through it   on
and on – from Romans to Christians, Moors to Visigoths,
Franco to Lorca, polling booths from right to left,
left to right, the winds of change breathing down our necks
as we traverse another hairpin bend in these –

Badlands, Madlands, Sadlands, Gladlands – full of festivals
and sun   and talk of racing drivers come undone.

We were in a Badlands bar when we heard the news –

scattered tables, stray cats and drifting music,
closing times that stretch like views and old tunes
carried on trays and ardent voices – wages frozen
like wind-farms in the heat,

austerity descending on the young and the
old and the weak – black money   diverted like
irrigation streams into the pockets of
politicians corrupted by greed –

the same songs – like a pattern – running over land
and air – and see – a solidarity of grim
yet familiar despair.

Later that night   I woke from sleep – full of racing
cars and motorbikes – Valentino – dressed as a
matador – stroking the ghost-grey dog of a grey-
hound stray that lived down the road between the church and
the bank and howled at the moon – with a strange
intelligence   to find – that it was...
and Valentino?
survived of another hoax   to live through the night
and emerge undead, raised from the grave to ride again

across these flat-lined, Badland lands – where a minister
stands in his prime on shifting sands   befuddled with
money and sleights of hand, counting his suits and
second flats to say:

'There   will   be   no   miracles.'

And the Badlands wait. Silent as rock. Slow as hills.
Safe as bones – secure in the knowledge that change
is inevitable.

The Venus Papers

Venus Arrives

What if Venus
the Roman goddess of love and beauty
washed up on a beach
in the 21st century?

Would she think of her mother,
Gaia, mamma mia,
would she think of her father,
Uranus, the great?

Would she remember how Cronus
her brother had taken
the sickle from Gaia
and castrated their dad?

No pun intended –
castrated Uranus?!
Would she remember how she
had been born

from the cut?

Venus Recalls

I was the first:
the woman –
even before Eve,
the first painted life-size,
eye for an eye,
knee for knee.

He painted me the seasons –
gave me his best,
body a pearl,
hair like a dress.

My legs were so much longer
than they ever were at sea.
My lips were so much redder
in the picture he could see.

He painted me like Twiggy
but paler than a page;
if my skin had been that ashen
we'd have been in a grave.

He made me like Athena,
head above the world,
neck like a swan,
features turned.

Snake-hipped vixen
impossibly shelled;
Venus/Adonis,
boy meets girl.

Venus at Customs (Interview with an Officer)

'Please state your country of origin.
Do you have a valid reason for leaving and for coming?
Do you believe your life to be in danger – or at risk of harm?'

Venus takes from out her purse a folded print of her arrival,
creases worn, cherubs hanging in the sky,
the likeness of her eyes – feet too small, but still.

'Have you been tortured or imprisoned?
Persecuted for any reason?
Do you believe your life to be in danger – or at risk of harm?'

She takes from out her purse: a photo taken when in Cyprus,
one from Florence, another Athens, then (from on the beach)
a postcard with a picture of a lighthouse.

They call for a translator.

'What is her country of origin?
Has she experienced persecution?
Does she believe her life to be in danger or at risk of harm?'

She says the sea is full of creatures,
that the water is undrinkable,
she talks about the night she nearly drowned –

and then about her mother and her brother –
the hit out on her father – the sickle and the killing
(she draws a careful picture on a piece of card).

The interviewing officer has heard it all before.

'WHAT – IS – YO-UR – COUN-TRY – OF – OR-I-GIN?
DO – YOU – HAVE – A – VAL-ID – REA-SON
FOR – LEA-VING – AND – FOR – COM-ING?'

The psychologist is uncertain.

The historian they call upon – cannot be sure.

There is – no passport.

'She cannot claim.
She must not work.
She cannot stay.
She must present herself
in fourteen days.'
They stamp each paper
with a scowl
and send her to
a gods-forsaken,
limbo-dwelling,
halfway, washed-out,
downtown
house.

Calling Venus

In the dark, dark forest
there was a dark, dark lane
and down the dark, dark lane
there was a dark, dark village
and from the dark, dark village
came a dark, dark town
and from the dark, dark town
came a dark, dark city
and in the dark, dark city
there was a dark, dark road
and on the dark, dark road
there was a bright, bright light
and by the bright, bright light
there was a tall, red box
and in the tall, red box
there was a black, black phone
and by the black, black phone
there was a pink, pink card
and on the pink, pink card
there was a short, short name
and the short, short name

was 'Venus'.

I dialled the number
beneath the name
and a ringtone rang,
a woman crooned
into my ear,

'Hello, this is Venus...'

I said,
'I'm Venus.'

She drawled,

'OK, "Venus"– what do you like?'

so I told her,

'Seagulls and razors
and... seamen... and crabs.'

There was silence on the line

and I could hear her breathe.
I fed her coins to keep her with me.

She told me – she was wet
so I asked,

'Are you in the sea?'

then she started to talk
about fingers and seams.
I just said nothing.
I didn't know where to go...

she growled,

'Are you there?'

and I nodded down the phone;

she groaned,

'Are you there?'

then began to moan.

I hung up the receiver
but rang straight back,
she called me a tease
and rattled a laugh –

then a car slid by,

then a woman with a man;
I curled a finger round the wire
and leant against the glass.

And she wanted me to come...
but I didn't know where.
She asked about my clothes –
I told her I was bare.

There was litter on the road
and her breath seemed to quicken.

There was a neon sign
and a guy in a tie
leaning from a window.

She told me I was bad
and I wanted to be better.

I said,

'Who are you?'

She said,

'Whoever.'

Things People Say about Venus in the Tabloids

You shouldn't be allowed to just sail into this country.
You can't just wash up in a shell and expect a hand-out.
We've all got our hard luck stories.
Bloody two-a-penny goddesses
coming down here, taking our jobs.
Go back to where you came from.
Nice tits.

Venus Walks into a Bar

'Venus, Venus,
every night the same thing –
you come in here – no money – no clothing,
then just stand there saying nothing
till I pour you a drink. It's bad for business.
Customers don't know what to make of it.
Strip bars they understand – but this?
Venus, baby, darling, please – you're killing me.'

      Venus stands there saying nothing,
      arms folded beneath her ribs,
      sheer feet glistening
      on the oak wood panelling.

'Look,' he says.
'If you're going to do it,
least you could do
is wear sequins.'

Venus Gets a Job as a Glamour Model

They ask her if no clothes
will be a problem. Venus says no –

she's used to it,
days at sea and not a stitch.

But they ask her to do
strange things;

touch herself all over
like she's trying to save her skin.

She tells them
that she's good with shells,

standing in one like a bell –
but the studio, it's got a style.

So she gets a deeper tan,
lifts her hair from gold to platinum.

The photographer adjusts a light,
lines a curve, peels a thigh,
tries to lift her breasts up high,

then passes her the card
of his favourite surgeon.

Venus Gets a Job as a Fashion Model

She wears clothes.
They are nice clothes –

like new skin but brighter,
like an advert for lipstick.

She learns
five ways to use her lips:

smile – with teeth, without,
lips ajar, smirk, pout.

The photographer says
the camera loves her.

Her agent says
she'd be a natural

if she could just
drop some weight.

Venus Meets a Mannequin

Someone has painted the mannequin gold
like the woman in the book
who got hit by her man:

Midas' girl.

She looks drawn;
stretched with hunger,
dressed in swimwear.

Venus – traces the line of her narrow torso,
presses a palm against the window,
mouths words –

'Are you in
any pain?
Is there anything
I can do?'

The golden girl
stares straight ahead.
Says – nothing.

Venus in Primark

Everything is so beautiful.
Venus has never seen anything like it;
rows and rows of crumpled silks,
woollen dresses, velvet heels.

She walks up aisles
like somebody getting married.
Mothers hold up jumpers
over leggings. Teenagers twirl

like vinyl records;
a queue of people
snakes a line
around the tills.

In a changing room
like the back of a wardrobe,
she presses a dress
against her body –

traces a seam
of fragile cotton,

wonders who made it.

Venus Goes Shopping

And the crowds spin round.
And the tower rises up.
And the clouds bear down.
And the tick and the tock.

I don't go home.
I stop in shops.
I try on clothes.
I wish and want.

And nothing really fits.
And everything I've got.
Another black vest.
Another dress around my throat.

Venus Votes

Her mother votes Green, is fond of the trees,
birds in her hair, leaves on her knees.
   Uranus votes Tory to try and appal her,
   pastes up their posters and flyers for free.
      Cherubs vote Labour, nymphs spoil the paper,
      sirens are curious but watch from the sea.
      Cyclopes are UKIP, Poseidon's for Liberals,
      Zeus for the workers, SWP.
The Fates change their mind a thousand times,
      Medusa stood – but didn't get in.
And she thinks of the booth, imagines the slip;
a Damocles pen conjures the ink.
   She stays up all night
   to hear the result,
   opinions land,
   policies roam.
Parliament hangs
   on
   a
   line
   of votes.

    Shall we all go to hell
    in a leaking boat?
   Do we all go to hell

  in a leaking boat?

```
  N      N      N      N      N        n
   n   n y   n y    n y    n y    n y   y n    y
 Y     Y     Y      Y       Y        n   yn n n
```

Venus Envy

Seagulls' feet around her eyes,
date of birth, another lie.
Venus stands inside a bar,
golden tresses burn like Mars.
She looks at girls – their gleaming hair,
amber arms, velvet stares.
Fishing lines around her neck,
checks her makeup, feels a wreck.
She shaves her legs with Venus razors,
dreams each night of glossy bathers.
And shadows creep across her cheeks
like the night falls on a beach.
Kate Moss poses with a shell
smiling like a Raphael.
Keira Knightley's on the telly
glowing like a Botticelli.

Venus Diets

It was nothing to write home about.
A brisk walk. A skipped meal.
She felt all right, just a little cold.

When she put a poster on her fridge,
Kate Moss like a starving seal,
it was nothing to write home about.

When she held a mirror to her mouth,
only apples, then only peel,
she felt all right, just a little cold.

She bought scales to weigh her bones,
wore flowing fabrics to conceal;
it was nothing to write home about.

It was for the best, she had no doubts;
the way to look, the way to feel.
She felt all right, just a little cold.

She collapsed at work, a paper doll.
In her car lost control of the wheel.
It was nothing to write home about.
She felt all right. Just a little cold.

Gaia

I saw her out on Holkham beach
shifting sand to set the scene;
marram like a lion's mane,
teasing roots to seal the grains.

I saw her skate a lunar queen
then shining silver on the trees,
in the first small town
she was weeds;
a dust cart's cloud
had her heat.

But it's been weeks
since she last wrote;
return to sender
she's not home.

She's out in Haiti screaming grief,
pouring rivers into seas.
There she is in Pakistan
in the waves, her arms, her back.

I see her on the TV screen
in the sun and birds and breeze.
I see her curled around a cloud,
I see her water falling down.

Gaia, Mother, Mother, Earth.
Where is the love?
Where is the nurse?

Gaia, Mother, Mother, Earth.
What have you done?
How is this earned?

Late at night, the moon a bone,
I call her on my lobster phone.
I listen to her singing tone.

Say nothing
to the answerphone.

Love Poem to Botticelli

Lying here beneath a sheet,
behind an open chink of sea –

a clearing – by a shaded tree,
mad with rum and darkened fields.

My spine's rolled inside your ghost.
You're the water. I'm the coast.

*

He sketched my hip like a line of horizon,
painted a wash like the tide coming in,
carded my back like a swept-away sand dune,
scribbled my feet like a couple of wings.

I took off my clothes like a jigsaw puzzle,
a Russian doll, piece by piece,
folded my skirt with a kung-fu tussle,
shook off the shoes like a flight of geese.

He was my Botticelli.
First and last.
Vulcan and Adonis.
Jupiter and Mars.

Man in the moon.
Man on the beach.
Off-stage lover.
Left behind me.

*

That night

their bodies pulled
like bright birds
from black bags.

But in morning he had gone
and she lay there in the sun
trembling.

Footprints

There are footprints on my wings
from where you cast me out;
shadow-black like coffee rings,
shadow-black, an admiral print.

There on my back
from where your foot,
there on my back,
pushed in its boot.

I wear your mud and dust like stripes.
I wrap them round my front at night.
Your writing's on my spine.
Your writing's down my sides.
Your cowboy soles are on my mind,
your footprints on my wings.

You said I was your favourite thing
that night we danced around the clouds,
you took my arms and spun me round
but there are footprints on my wings.

You said you thought the earth had moved
when I walked in and round a room,
you said I made the heavens sing
but there are footprints on my wings.

Last week I saw a woman stare,
her look like pity opened bare.
I can't wear glasses on my back.
I can't disguise your blue and black,
your footprints on my wings.

There in Sainsbury's by the veg
I saw her look and look again,
like underneath her clothes
there might be footprints on her bones.

But every day they fade some more,
purple kisses, dimming thoughts
and every night I sponge them down
and water runs like feelings drowned,
your footprints from my wings.

I can't keep coming back for more
now the marks are not so raw.

If she and I could leave today
like all the marks, just fade away,
we'd walk with wishbones, never say
that there were footprints on our wings.
There'd be no footprints on our wings.
No more footprints on our wings.

Incanto

What if you could cast a spell
and turn the sand dunes into homes?
Boats to castles, rope to pearl,
rocks to rubies, stones to sails.
Scales would be clothes
to wear in the winter,
nets would be ball-gowns,
mussels to drink from.
Fishing lines would be words from a treaty;
seaweed – a bed, seagulls – children.
Skeletons mobiles to hang from a cradle;
driftwood – a lover,
pine trees – angels.
What if you could cast a spell
and all the sand would be rice
and coconuts shoes
grass would be blankets,
litter – food?
What if you could cast a spell
and all our thoughts would be bells?
What if you could cast a spell
and all our landmines would be shells?

Educating Venus

After Malala Yousafzai and Rudyard Kipling

The first lesson – is that seeking a lesson
may teach you a lesson.

In the school yard in Paktia
the water in the well
may be poisoned.

On the school bus in Mingora
there may be Semtex
beneath the seats.

The second lesson – they may come for you
on the streets of Swat in your daiquiri sari,
forbidden colours, modest hour   glass of strawberry.

The third lesson – you may hide in the cupboard;
you may take off your shoe and wield it as a weapon.

The fourth lesson – resort to reason, return to sender
scarlet letters gloating guilt.

The fifth lesson – bodies hanging on a traffic island.
In Pakistan a girl is flogged
for attempting trigonometry,
for number and naming the bones in a foot.

The sixth lesson – three bullets, red on the leather
pale and pleated as a scalloped shell.

The seventh lesson – dried on the lino,
swimming past seats and down the aisle.

The eighth lesson – blood, blood
puddled in shoes, soaked into socks,
filling up bags and the pages of books.

The ninth lesson – you may not drive.
You may not learn the highway code.
In Saudi Arabia a cleric warns
how leaning forward to change a gear
will crush the ovaries and kill a child.

The tenth lesson – and Mercedes-Benz
bends a set of dislocated breasts
around a wheel – for the sake of selling cars
shoots a line of headless female body parts.

American Apparel – exemplifies
objectify – spreads nylon legs like butter
to testify an utter lack of love.

Online a woman dies
eleven thousand troll-knifed lies
for asking for her head upon a bank note.
The twelfth lesson –

Ugly sisters cut off their toes
and bunions and callouses
to make them fit
into Cinderella slippers
of gossamer and gold,
made of glass and grass
and squirrel fur,
but when it doesn't work
are made by the prince
and a gaggle of hens
to wear red-hot iron boots
and dance themselves to death.

The thirteenth lesson –

If you can keep your knees together
when all about you there are others parting theirs.

If you can walk the walk of Babylon
and shun or screw all shouts of 'slut' or 'whore'.

If you can raise a child
and run a household like a country

or choose to work
and feel no lack for lacking kids.

If you can gather in Kabul inside a room
and whisper poems when verses are forbidden.
If you can phone in words suppressed by governments,
feed lines like vines down wires, crackling with silence.

If you can stand and shatter ceilings with your rising
or bang your head and not be forced to sit.

If you can fail and not be put off for the losing.
If you can win and not feel guilt or undermine the thing.

If you can be yourself and not the product in the advert.
If you can age with grace or gracelessly.
If you can be whatever in the mist you might imagine.
If you can be both bad and good
and more than fifty shades of in-between.

If you can choose to live however best befits you
and disregard all lists – and the lecturing of – if,

then, my dear – you'll be a woman.
You'll be a woman   –   zen   زَن
عورت   oarat
şch   ښځه .

85

Venus Leaves

You can stay too long.
It wasn't that she hated it,
just missed the mermaids
and the rocks.

And it wasn't what she had expected
though she never meant to buy;
the celebrities were beautiful
but sad around the eyes.

Sometimes, late at night
she lights a candle in her shell,
imagines that she never left,
drifts with a terrace
floating on the waves.

She dreams about the island,
that she married, had a child,
that they walked each day in the country
then fell asleep side by side.

Sometimes she unfolds an advert
brought back with her as a souvenir;
she gazes at the model like a statue,
gently touches her tumbling hair.

And the rain falls down on the seafront,
moon falls down from the sky;
she dreams about going back there
but this time being Venus;
this time, not having to lie.

Prayer

Our Mother who art in oceans,
Hallowed be thy scales.
Thy seabed come;
I will be done
On earth
As I was in water.
Give us our fishnets
And forgive us our dresses
As we forgive those
Who dress against us,
And lead us not into starvation
But deliver us from diets
And shopping and surgery,
Deliver us from customs
And Primark and purgery,
For ours is the longing
Of all generations,
Ours is the wanting
And needing
And staving.
For ever and ever
Our daughters of Hades.
For ever and ever
Our Lady,
Our ladies.
For ever and ever
Our sisters,
Our children.
For ever and ever,
Amen.

Thanks and Acknowledgements

I would like to thank my family: Sarah and Michael Towsey; Bandi bácsi; parents, Margaret and Paul Towsey and partner, Scott Bridgwood in particular for their stories, love and support. Thanks too to Scott for his continuous inspiration, feedback, assistance – and of course, this book's cover.

The Venus Papers title sequence was first edited and directed by Jean Binta Breeze MBE whose friendship, advice and collaboration have had an enormous impact on both me and my work; blessings to her elbow and via phone-lines, her veranda. I would like to thank the late mark.s (aka, 'the ghost poet') for 15 years of weekly coffee, closeness, poetry swapping and deep debate.

Acknowledgements are due to the editors of the following places and publications in which some of these poems first appeared: *Hearing Voices* (Crystal Clear Press), *The London Magazine*, *Grassroutes Writers Gallery* (University of Leicester), *The Coffee House* (Charnwood Arts), *The Stare's Nest* and *Hallelujah for 50ft Women* (Bloodaxe Books).

Alice was written in response to IFEA (International Festival of Emerging Artists) a two week residency with Theatre Royal Stratford East in 2008. *Tawanda* was commissioned by Apples and Snakes in 2009 as part of *Beyond Words* – a UK tour of five South African poets: Donata Mattera, Lesego Rampolokeng, Phillippa Yaa de Villiers, Lebo Mashile and South African Poet Laureate, Keorapetse Kgositsile. *Miss Havisham's House* was commissioned by Leicester Museum Service. *The Don't Look Dance* was written in preparation for a performance at Marie Fidelis School, commissioned by Poet in City in 2011.

I am extremely grateful to Arts Council England for grants awarded in 2009 and 2014. These enabled me to write and refine many of the poems featured within *The Venus Papers* title sequence and other poems in this collection produced for *Three the Hard Way – Part One* (www.3thehardwaypoets.wordpress.com) UK tour with Jean Binta Breeze and Alison Dunne in 2014.

Thanks to a number of people and organisations for much appreciated help and encouragement, including: Julia Bird, Jaybird Productions; Michael Horovitz, New Departures, Jazz Poetry SuperJams and Poetry Olympics; Rob Gee; Henderson Mullen, Writing East Midlands; Sarah Ellis, Apples and Snakes; Melanie Abrahams, renaissance one; Jo Ivie, Poet in the City; Mahendra Solanki and David Belbin, Nottingham Trent University, Creative Writing MA Programme and Clive Birnie plus all at Burning Eye Books.